"Lynn's *Six Word Lessons to Take the Fear Out of Mortgages* is the perfect book for anyone considering buying a home. Lynn offers her mortgage expertise by sharing the most important aspects of qualifying for a home loan. This quick and easy read not only highlights the entire loan and home buying process, but also provides tips on how to ensure it results in a smooth and successful closing. One of the qualities I admire most about Lynn is her heartfelt passion for helping single women qualify for a home loan. She believes knowledge is power, which inspires action. Home ownership is attainable, especially when buyers are educated." **--Dana V. Adams, Managing Broker, Windermere Real Estate, Kirkland, Washington**

"Lynn is definitely an expert in her field and has managed with this book to simplify what can sometimes be a complicated and stressful process. Her love for what she does and her passion to help each and every customer she works with realize their dreams comes out in the chapters of this little gem, a must-read for anyone purchasing a home!" **--Ilana Yagudayev, American Family Insurance**

"They say it takes a village to raise a child. It also takes a village to buy a home, especially if you are a first-time homeowner or single person. Along with having a trusted Realtor by your side, on your other side should be a trusted mortgage lender, like Lynn Reifert. My faith in Lynn has grown strong over the years because she is tenacious, determined, caring, creative, resourceful and quite frankly, knows her stuff! There is no perfect transaction and hurdles and challenges are bound to come your way, but if you have a great team leading you, and Lynn at the mortgage helm, the odds of catching your dream home will be fantastic." **--Beth Phillips-York, Realtor, TeamBuilder Keller Williams**

"This book is a great primer for anyone yearning to buy a home. Lynn takes you through all the steps and explains the terms which may seem confusing. Lynn helps people who are divorced, going through divorce, or just thinking about it. This book will help you make good decisions that will help you get into your dream home and start a new future." **--Karin Quirk, Attorney at Law, DivorceforGrownups.net**

"Lynn has made the loan process easier to understand by breaking down the steps and explaining them to the borrower in a logical way. From application to closing of a sale or refinance, if you want to make educated, step by step decisions, use the lender that has years of 'around the block' experience walking borrowers through the process." **-- Teresa K. Nelson (aka Teresa Fabulous) Windermere Real Estate, Woodinville, Washington**

"This is a fabulous book for anyone who is just starting the home buying process. It can also be very beneficial to those who haven't purchased in a long time, and need a refresher course." **--Lesa Say, Realtor, Re/Max**

Six-Word Lessons to

TAKE THE FEAR
OUT OF MORTGAGES

100 Lessons to Realize Your
Dream of Home Ownership

Lynn Reifert

Published by Pacelli Publishing
Bellevue, Washington

SIX
~WORD
LESSONS

Six-Word Lessons to Take the Fear Out of Mortgages

Published by Pacelli Publishing
9905 Lake Washington Blvd. NE, #D-103
Bellevue, Washington 98004
PacelliPublishing.com

Cover and interior designed by Pacelli Publishing
Author photo by Nikki Closser Photography
Cover image by AdobeStock

ISBN-10: 1-933750-77-4
ISBN-13: 978-1-933750-77-4

Dedication

To my husband Fred for being so very supportive in whatever I choose to do. Even when he has no idea how I'll do it – he trusts that I will make it happen! To my two sons that I am so incredibly proud of, Nick and Jamie – thanks for being uniquely you. You will always be my babies. To my sister Jennifer, I'm very thankful to have you in my life and you're stuck with me! Love you all!

To my parents in heaven, Mom and Dad -- I wish you were still here with us. I choose to believe that you see everything that is happening and are proud of your family. I am so thankful that you raised me to believe I could do ANYTHING I wanted to do if I just worked hard and kept at it, and I DO! ☺

You were right, and I miss you every day.

"Now faith is confidence in what we hope for and assurance about what we do not see."

Hebrews 11:1 NIV

Table of Contents

A Note from Lynn

I've helped so many people finance their own homes. Many of these people thought it would never happen for them. They paid some bills a week late and thought they'd have horrible credit. They finally let me pull credit and two months later were in their own home. Don't be afraid to ASK. I wrote this book because I wanted to help people to not be afraid to start the process and find out! I'd love to hear your thoughts and would appreciate a review on Amazon.com!

Contact me through LynnReifert.com or email FearFreeMortgage@gmail.com

I hope you are moved to find out more about buying YOUR own home! ☺

Lynn

Lessons I've Learned During this Process

1

What makes a person take action?

For me it was writing this book. I wanted to be able to give something to my clients, to help them see the full process of getting a mortgage loan. But more than that I wanted them to know how much I genuinely care about them, specifically about them becoming homeowners. I could give them someone else's book, but I knew that wouldn't really get MY message across. I knew I would have to write it myself.

2

Who am I drawn to help?

There are two main groups that have my heart. One group is first-time homebuyers, and the other is single women. They need someone they can fully trust to walk them through this process. I absolutely love being that person. Once they become homeowners on their own they know that NOTHING is impossible, and the future looks brighter. That is the best compensation for the work I do.

3

Who are my favorite past clients?

As I was writing the book, I had the idea to ask a few of my past clients if they'd be willing to share what they learned through the process. Did they have any advice for someone who was in the spot they had been in previously – thinking they would never become homeowners? The response was more than I expected and I hope their messages inspire you!

4

Getting a mortgage can change lives.

Getting a mortgage can change lives. I see it over and over. I remember how much my husband and I wanted to own our own home, and I bring that feeling with me to every loan I handle. I hope these 100 Lessons inspire you and take the fear out of mortgages, whether it's your first home, or the first home on your own!

Budgeting: How Much Can You Afford?

5

Personal budget - why you need one!

It is so important that you create your own budget before even considering buying a house. You need to know what you really have left over after taxes and after your survival costs. Your lender will only be looking at the expenses on the credit report. It's up to you to know that you can comfortably afford the new payment!

6

What can you afford for housing?

I often hear people say they'll have no problem paying $800 more for a mortgage than they currently pay for rent. I'll ask how much they've been saving each month. My advice is to start saving the additional amount you'll need for the mortgage payment now. Then you will KNOW you can afford it, and you'll have more money saved. Be sure to discuss mortgage insurance options if you are putting less than 20 percent down.

7

Do you anticipate any new expenses?

While creating your budget, keep in mind any upcoming expenses. Do you pay your car insurance monthly or every six months? Be sure to anticipate vacations, holidays, slow periods at work if you receive a bonus, and commission or overtime income. Plan for unexpected expenses. Your car will eventually break down. Plan for that by saving some of your money from every paycheck.

8

Include these items in your budget.

How much do you spend each month for basic survival? When creating your budget, make sure you include the following items: food, gas, car insurance, utilities, cable, internet, cell phone, haircut, nails, daycare, occasional gifts, Christmas, vacations, etc. What are some other expenses you would need to include in your budget?

9

You'll need to budget for repairs.

Once you are a homeowner, if something breaks or needs updating, it is all on you. It will be very important to budget for repairs and save for future expenses. Eventually the roof will need to be replaced, along with the gutters, furnace and many other things. You'll want to keep the habit of saving going even after your home loan closes. Start now and it will be painless.

10

Save money on lunch and coffee.

Some of the quickest ways to save money are to make your own lunches, and make your coffee at home. Going to coffee shops can add up quickly, and so can eating out or ordering food. Keep track of how much you are spending on these things and I'll bet you'll be able to buy your own espresso maker in no time!

11

In debt? The snowball method works.

To use the "snowball" method you list your debts from lowest to the highest balance. Pay at least the minimum payment on everything. Say that your first bill has a $20 payment. Once that balance is paid off, you take that $20 and add it to the payment due for the second bill. Keep doing that until you have paid off everything.

12

Does interest matter when paying debts?

Some people say to pay off debts with the highest interest first, rather than the lowest balance. If you do it both ways in a snowball tool, you'll find that you might save one month by doing it that way. I would rather pay a few of the lower bills quickly to gain momentum. Go with whatever appeals to you.

13

Free online budgeting resources that help

You can find free budgeting and snowball tools online, as well as several books and programs for purchase. A simple Excel spreadsheet will work. Use whatever you need to start tracking your expenses to know exactly where your money is going, and how much you can really afford to put toward a house payment. Save all your receipts for a month or two so you can track how much you are really spending.

Credit Score – Rip the Band-Aid Off!

14

Do you know your credit score?

There are several free credit scoring sources, but they are not a replacement for finding out what your actual credit scores are. A full mortgage credit report will contain all three scores from Equifax, Experian and TransUnion. Most of the free models have some version of scoring that is uniquely their own. These scores don't do anything for you when you are seeking your actual scores.

15

"I don't want a hard inquiry."

In order to get a loan preapproval, a lender will have to pull their own credit report. Yes, this will be a "hard inquiry." But if pulling your credit is going to make that much difference in your credit score, there is probably more work needed anyway. This is where I say, "It is what it is, so let's rip the Band-Aid off so you know, and then I can help you from there."

16

Your credit score is a snapshot.

Your credit scores are a snapshot of what the bureaus are currently reporting the moment the report is pulled. Credit inquiries, late payments, new collections and loan balances can cause your scores to change. Creditors typically report once a month, so you will see information based on the last reporting. If you have time to pay off or pay down some of your lowest balances, your score may be higher.

17

Yes, you can raise your score.

The quickest way to raise your credit score is to pay down your balances. Being maxed out will raise your score, but keeping the balance to less than thirty percent of your loan limit will help raise your score. Make sure if you are an authorized user that the account is being paid on time, and balance is under thirty percent of the credit limit.

18

Basic rules regarding your credit score.

The best way to keep your scores consistent is to make sure you are making payments on time each month. Don't go over the limit, and don't become past due on any accounts. Collections will affect your score less and less the older they get. Don't pay older accounts off without talking to your lender first.

19

How a Rescore report benefits you.

A Rescore report is a faster way to get credit changes updated. Since creditors report monthly, and typically toward the end of the month, it could take over a month to see the change in credit score. For a Rescore, I receive proof of the change from you, and get the Rescore within a week. The lender can't charge you for this service.

20

How does a bankruptcy affect scores?

Having a bankruptcy does affect your credit scores, but often not as badly as someone with lots of late payments and unpaid collections. Once the bankruptcy is discharged, with improved, minimal use of credit, you will see the scores start to rebound. Within two or three years of discharge you should be eligible to buy, if you have rebuilt credit.

21

Credit score will affect your rate.

Anything at 740 or above is considered Excellent credit and you will receive the best rate pricing. Over 700 is still considered very good, while anything under 640 may need to be worked on a bit to see if it can be improved to raise the score. There are programs that will work for scores of 620, and sometimes even down to 580.

Choosing Your Lender and Realtor Wisely

22

Questions you need to be asking.

An experienced lender and agent (or Realtor) will save you money and stress. Your agent represents you and will negotiate with the other agent on your behalf. You want experience and someone who is not only good with the numbers but one who takes the time to find out what your future plans are, so that they structure your loan in a way that works for you now, and in the future.

23

Is the agent familiar with location?

Be sure that your agent is familiar with the areas you are interested in. You want the agent to know what is on the market, and how one house compares to another in order to negotiate properly and know what is available as well as what's happening in the local area. It's not necessary that they be an expert, but the more familiar they are, the more helpful they will be to you.

24

Are you comfortable asking them questions?

This relationship is important. You will most likely be spending a lot of time with them. You want to know that they have your back, and you want to feel comfortable asking them questions, knowing they will take the time to answer and explain in a way that makes sense to you. If you ever need a referral for an agent, just let me know - I know several!

25

Will they be available to you?

Most lenders and agents expect that you will need help after hours and will work to be available as much as possible, but please respect their time too. If your 10 p.m. phone call can wait until 10 a.m., I know they will appreciate it! Also, if you go to a local bank or credit union for financing, you won't be getting a preapproval letter over the weekend, in most cases.

26

Did you read their customer reviews?

Read reviews on their website and on Zillow. Five stars are nice, but look at how people describe them. Look for key words describing traits that are important to you. When I look at reviews I'm looking for "proactive" and "she cared about us" as well as "experienced" and "no-nonsense." Think about what you want. Add your own review once your transaction is complete. We appreciate those reviews more than you know!

27

Trust your choice and commit now.

You want to be able to trust that your lender and agent have your best interest in mind – not theirs. If you feel like you have a good match, then commit to them so you can put your energy and focus into finding the right house, and the right loan program that fits your financial needs and goals. A lot of time is wasted shopping for the best rate or the agent that will cut their fee. Never forget that you get what you pay for.

28

It's about more than interest rate.

We select doctors based on their knowledge and how they make us feel. We want to know they care about our health and healing. With your lender, it is very important that they know what they're doing, and that they care that your loan closes on time. The rates you see quoted online are rarely accurate. Read the small print to see if points are being charged for that crazy low rate.

Preapproval Letters - Why They are Necessary

29

Their importance to you and seller.

Your preapproval letter confirms how much you are preapproved to buy, along with the loan program and required down payment. This can be less than twenty percent. Ask your lender what your options are. This assures you that you can go into contract knowing that you are preapproved by your lender. It also assures the seller and agent that they can accept your offer, knowing you are qualified to purchase the home.

30

What is a full credit preapproval?

If there are any concerns with your loan approval, I highly advise that you ask your lender to submit your file for a fully underwritten credit approval. This gives everyone peace of mind that both the loan consultant and underwriter have reviewed your information. If you are self-employed, have multiple streams of income or have had a few job gaps in the last few years, definitely get the full credit approval.

31

Will your lender call the agent?

One thing that is helpful for buyers is to have their lender call the listing agent. Confirming you are qualified, easy to work with and quick to respond may give you the edge over competing offers. The lender's reputation is crucial. I love when listing agents says, "Oh, your company has an excellent reputation and I know it will close on time!" It's clear they don't receive these calls on every offer.

32

Type of loan should be noted.

The letter needs to state which loan program you are preapproved for. Anything other than a Conventional loan may be viewed as less desirable due to appraisal requirements or longer underwriting time, but your agent can usually negotiate with compensating factors in your favor. An experienced lender will know how to perform no matter which program you have, and keep things moving smoothly.

33

Down payment assistance programs: fine print

My favorite down payment assistance program in Washington state is WSHFC.org. I teach the classes and am very familiar with the program. If you use another program, please be sure to read ALL the fine print. Many have fees or penalties that may not affect you until years later. Nothing is free – always do your own research.

34

Local lender or a big bank?

A big bank may sometimes have better rates, but they typically have longer closing timelines, frustration in reaching your loan officer and difficulty with getting preapproval over the weekend. I find that those of us who work for mortgage companies tend to be more available and more relational – but I am biased! I stay in touch with clients and I invite them to client events after closing too.

35

Seller credit -do you need one?

A seller credit is a certain dollar amount or percentage of the sales price that can (only) be used toward your closing costs or prepaids. You can never get cash back at closing from the seller. Conventional is three percent and FHA is six percent maximum. If you have extra credit, you will lose it if it's not applied to costs. Get a premium warranty, buy down the rate – but use it all!

36

Will you be getting a gift?

A "gift" refers to funds received from a family member, close friend or employer. There are specific requirements for gifts, so be sure to let your lender and agent know you are receiving gift funds. The donor will need to complete a "gift letter," a bank statement, and a paper trail of the transfer of funds. It's important this is handled properly to avoid a delay in closing.

37

Closing costs - make sure you know!

Your lender should provide a fee estimate that shows your expected closing costs. Your earnest money deposit will be applied toward the amount due at closing – as well as any seller credits that have been agreed upon. There should be no surprises about this and if you don't understand, it is important that you ask until you are clear on the approximate amount you are expected to bring in at closing.

Ten Forbidden Actions During Loan Process

38

Please do not do these things.

In this chapter I will go into detail regarding several things you can't do while you are in the loan process. We often refer to them as the Ten Commandments because they are that important and can cause your purchase to come to a screeching halt. Please make sure you understand the importance of this section!

39

Don't open any new credit cards.

New accounts will ding your credit score because they will lack history. Don't apply for any credit during this time. You don't want to close any accounts either. Don't apply for any "fast cash" loans and if you have any – pay them off. Get out of that cycle before even thinking of buying a house! Keep paying all bills on time and don't let anything become past due or go to collections. Buy appliances and furniture after closing.

40

Don't even use your credit cards.

While you are in the loan process, it is better to refrain from using your credit cards. Most lenders have a monitoring system that will alert underwriting if you open new accounts, or if your current balance increases, which will also increase your payments. Be aware of any increase in payments due to interest-free periods ending. Additional payments will raise your debt to income ratio.

41

Don't quit your current job yet.

Please do not quit your job, or even give notice. Do not decide to become self-employed, go to a straight-commission situation, or make any changes to the way you are currently paid. If for some reason you have to make a job change, tell your lender as soon as possible and make sure it is in the same line of work, and at or above your current pay. If the new pay is anything but salary, you may have issues.

42

Don't touch the money you've saved!

Make sure that you leave your savings account alone. If you get to the end of the process and are short on funds to close, your loan won't close and you will lose the house. You may be able to scramble to get a gift from a relative, but it will slow down closing and it will become very stressful for all involved. Just don't touch the savings account!

43

Do not buy any motor vehicles.

Please refrain from buying a new car, your dream boat or the RV you've had your eye on. Buying anything that will show up on credit may put your loan approval at risk. The new payment will need to be figured into your ratios. It may not be an issue if your ratios are low enough, but it will be a hassle for you to document the new payment. It is much better to wait until after closing.

44

Don't forget to disclose other debts.

You may have debts that aren't on your credit report. These will usually be discovered. It's better to provide your lender with the information up front. You may have a timeshare or maybe you own a piece of property that is paid off, but you pay taxes on it. These are expenses that need to be added into your debt ratio so it's best to address it up front.

45

Beware of making those cash deposits!

Cash deposits have caused more grief than almost anything else other than someone quitting their job. Cash deposits need to be documented. This is definitely true for large deposits, but what constitutes a large deposit changes. I advise you to always check with your lender before making a cash deposit. If possible, just keep the cash and use it for your living expenses.

46

Don't switch banks during this process.

Whatever your bank has done to make you mad – don't leave them until the loan has closed. If you do you will need to document the whole thing with statements from the old account and the new account. It's just one more thing that can be avoided by waiting until your loan closes.

47

Don't cosign a loan for anyone.

Cosigning a loan is the same thing as if it was only your loan. Whatever happens, be it late payments, repossession, or increase of the original limit – it's all going to be reported on your credit report. If that person stops making payments, the creditor will come after you. Just say no! If you cosign, we have to count that debt unless we can document the other party has made all payments (usually for at least twelve months).

48

Advice on planning your upcoming vacation.

Plan vacations for after you buy your new house. It will be much smoother on you and everyone else if you are in town during the process. Save the vacation for after closing when you'll be able to really relax. If you have travel plans that can't be changed (a wedding, or Grandma's birthday) please make sure all parties are made aware as early as possible.

House Shopping -Now the Fun Starts!

49

Your Realtor is your best advocate.

You have your preapproval letter in hand, and you are ready to shop for your future home! Your Realtor or agent is the one you will lean on for possible issues, and to point out positive features of houses. With each house you look at, you'll become more aware of what you really want. This can be a very stressful time, but it is also a lot of fun, so enjoy the process!

50

Your agent negotiates on your behalf.

Keep in mind that your agent negotiates on your behalf – and watches out for your best interest. If you go to an open house, you should still call your own agent if you want to make an offer. Your agent does many things behind the scenes that you may not even be aware of, so I highly advise that you use an agent whether buying or selling a property.

51

Who does the listing agent represent?

The listing agent represents the seller. While a buyer can have the listing agent represent them too, I don't advise it. Most agents will usually refer a buyer out to another agent so they aren't in this position, but you want to be aware. You will probably be going to open houses, and if you already have an agent you're working with, just let them know that.

52

Don't move the furniture just yet!

Do your best to not get emotionally attached – easier said than done! From the time you put an offer in until the time the loan closes, many things can go wrong. The inspections may come back with a deal-breaking issue for you. The underwriter may calculate income differently. The point is, don't mentally move yourself into this home until your loan closes and you will save yourself a lot of heartache.

53

Multiple offers and your loan type.

I touched a little on this earlier, but your loan type usually won't really matter if there are only a few interested in the home. If you are competing with ten other offers, maybe some of them cash offers, it will make it a lot more difficult to get an offer accepted. Your agent will guide you through this and your lender will give you options based on their view of your financial situation.

54

It's really true – location, location, location!

The sales price will be higher in a major city versus in the suburbs. Good schools and access to major stores and attractions also raise desirability. Many are finding they need to stretch their search to find homes in their price range. Get the best home you can afford, in the best location, at a price you can comfortably manage.

55

Home warranties are a good option.

Sometimes the seller or the buyer's agent will cover a home warranty, but if not, I highly recommend that you purchase one if you can. A home warranty can cover a variety of items, and save you from having to replace a furnace, refrigerator or maybe a dishwasher in your first year of living in your home. They come in a variety of options, so ask your agent for a recommendation of which warranties are available in your area.

Home Inspections, Insurance, Flood and More

56

Other details you need to know.

Buying a home will most likely be the biggest purchase you will make. It is a huge commitment and you want to be sure you are making a good investment. Your Realtor will be your first ally in this, along with the lender and other vendors we'll discuss in the next few pages. There are many types of inspections. Following are just a few.

57

What does the appraiser look at?

The appraiser's job is to determine the current value of the property. The appraiser will find comparable houses to determine the value, based on recent nearby comparables. The appraiser will also note anything that may be a safety concern (no rails on a deck) or areas that need attention (FHA appraisers will require peeling paint to be scraped and repainted, for example). Prices vary depending on type of loan and property.

58

What does the home inspector do?

The home inspector is hired by the buyer to do a full inspection of the home for any issues inside or outside. Usually they charge per square foot, but prices will vary. Your agent will know of home inspectors they trust. The inspector will spend a few hours going over every part of the house and will provide you with a full report. Please always get a home inspection.

59

Is a pest inspector needed too?

Your home inspector may note if a pest inspection should be done. They are not always needed, except that currently they are required for VA loans. A pest inspection will be an additional expense to the buyer, but worth it so you know what you are getting into. My suggestion is to find a home inspector who is also a licensed pest inspector – and cover both with one fee!

60

Information on sewer and septic inspections

A sewer is connected to the city's water source, and a septic is your own private system, located in your backyard. Your agent will be your best source of information on what is required for each. This is really a case by case situation, and just be aware that there may be additional requirements or inspections needed to make sure that the sewer (or the septic) is functioning properly.

61

Lead-based paint information for you

The federal government banned the use of lead-based paint in 1978, but homes newer than 1978 can still contain lead-based paint. If you have any questions on this it is best to discuss with your real estate agent.

62

Wood-burning fireplaces and chimney inspections

If the home has a wood-burning fireplace it is a good idea to get a chimney inspection. Some older chimneys don't have flue liners, or the brick inside the chimney may be crumbling. A chimney inspector will also make sure smoke is discharged properly and that no animals are living in it. This can also be done after closing.

63

Deciding on your home insurance agent

When it comes to home insurance, do not decide by price alone. It is very important that you have the proper coverage on your home and auto. For this reason, I strongly advise you to use a specific agent, rather than an 800 phone number or online quote. If something happens, do you want to talk to an agent who knows you, or to a computer? I have a few agents that I recommend and trust, so ask me.

64

Flood insurance: Do you need it?

Some locations will obviously need flood insurance, and your agent will be aware. But other times it won't become known until the appraiser checks it as a flood zone on the appraisal. The lender will always check to see if it's in a flood zone too. If it is, you will be required to buy flood insurance, which can be expensive, because the first year is required to be paid upfront.

Loan Submission – What Is the Process?

65

Here's where it gets really real!

Once you've found a house, signed off on the inspection, have the appraisal done and the initial title report is in, your loan is prepared to go to the underwriter. Underwriters are very good at coming up with a few more items that you'll need to provide, so be prepared for that. Work quickly to provide any additional items to keep the process moving along. Stay positive and keep packing.

66

Here's some mortgage lingo for you.

The following lessons will explain some terms you will need to know. Mortgage has its own language, like most other industries. Always remember to ask if you have a question, or if you are unclear about something. I would much rather have someone ask lots of questions than to find out at the end they were afraid to ask!

67

Does "escrow" mean two different things?

"Escrow" or "escrow" does refer to two different things. One being the Escrow office – a physical location where you will sign the loan documents, unless you sign somewhere else with a notary. The other "escrow" refers to an escrow account. This is set up in the new mortgage so that the payments are included in your mortgage payment, the home insurance is paid yearly by the mortgage company, and taxes are paid twice a year.

68

Approved with conditions – get to work!

Once you are notified that you are "approved with conditions," it is time to get to work, and we will start gathering any additional items the underwriter has asked for. This could be verification of a large deposit, or anything that will help the underwriter to tie it all together so they can give us "final approval."

69

What does "Clear to Close" mean?

Clear to Close means that the underwriter has signed off on all the conditions and now we are ready to order your loan documents! Once you get to this part it should be smooth sailing and you will probably sleep better than you have in weeks, knowing that the scrutiny period is over and you're almost there!

Loan Approval and Moving Toward Closing

70

You've received loan approval, now what?

This is the exciting part! Now you know for sure that the underwriter has approved you, based on meeting the conditions listed on the approval. Work quickly with your lender and processor to get those conditions in as soon as possible. Be aware that when you send conditions in, the underwriter may need further clarification, so be ready to send more until you hear that everything has been signed off.

71

Commit to your insurance agent now.

If you haven't already committed to which insurance agent you'll use, now is the time to get that done. We will need to order an Insurance Binder so that we have the exact annual premium. This affects your payment so please make sure this is done quickly if it hasn't already been decided.

72

Letters of explanation - why so many?

You may have to write several Letters of Explanation in order to explain job gaps, large bank deposits, credit inquiries, past addresses – anything the underwriter feels is not completely clear already. The letters help to tie up any loose ends and are completely normal, so don't be concerned. Just do your best in explaining and be sure to sign and date it.

73

Get your conditions in right away.

Once you've been given the list of underwriting conditions be sure to get them in as soon as possible. Every day counts in this process and if you want to meet your close date, be sure to do everything in your power to keep things moving forward. If you have a question on any of the items be sure to get the answer right away so you can start working on it and get it to your loan processor or loan consultant within 24 hours, if possible.

74

Go ahead and set up utilities.

Now is a good time to contact the utility companies to schedule the cancellation date for your current house and the installation date for the new one. Make sure when cancelling your current accounts that you allow for your cleanout period, so you aren't cleaning in the dark.

75

Your closing date has been confirmed.

At this time, your lender should be able to confidently confirm that everything is on track for closing and confirm that you will close on time (always the #1 goal!) and that you can start planning for the move. Just to be safe, make sure you know the moving truck's cancellation policies. You never know if something may happen to delay and you want to be prepared.

76

What is the Closing Disclosure/CD?

Usually within ten days of closing, you will receive your CD or Closing Disclosure by email. This will detail all the fees and terms of your loan, so that you have a clear picture of what you are paying and how much money you'll need to bring to escrow. Once you sign this, the "3 day clock" begins and if documents are ready, you will be able to sign after the third day. Once the loan has closed, you will get the Final CD.

77

Can I schedule the moving truck?

Wait until the CD has been signed, conditions cleared and your lender gives you the okay before scheduling movers. Check with your agent to be sure you are clear on your date of occupancy; when you can officially move in. This may be the same day as the closing, or a later date. It will be noted on the first page of your purchase contract. Make sure you are clear on this before scheduling a truck or movers.

Final Approval, Funding and Post Closing

78

Final approval – now we're ordering docs!

Once we have received your final approval, meaning that all the conditions have been signed off by the underwriter, the loan processor can order your loan documents. At this point the loan goes into the final audit to make sure that nothing has been missed. Once cleared it moves on to the "docs drawing" stage.

79

Draw the loan documents now please!

At this time the closing department prepares your loan documents, making sure your names and all terms of the loan are spelled out correctly. Currently all loan documents are signed by hand instead of Docusign, but we are getting closer and closer to using Docusign. Once the documents are prepared they are emailed to the Escrow office.

80

Loan documents have arrived at escrow.

Oh happy day! This is probably the moment all parties sigh a breath of relief! Once the documents are at escrow I think everyone finally relaxes, knowing the finish line is near. Once the Escrow office received the documents, they print and prepare them and set an appointment with you to come in to sign, or they can usually set an appointment with a notary to meet you.

81

Escrow appointment to sign your documents.

Be sure you bring current ID to your appointment. Ask whether they require a cashier's check, or if you'll need to wire the funds directly to escrow. They can't accept personal checks. Always make sure you have the exact amount needed, or more if you want to have a cushion. They will refund any extra funds back to you after closing.

82

Signed documents sent back to lender

Now that the documents have been signed, the escrow officer will send the signed loan documents back to the lender's funding department. The funder will review carefully to make sure everything has been signed and any funding conditions have been met. Once everything is satisfied, on close date the funder will send the wire to escrow.

83

Am I closed once it's funded?

"Your loan has funded!" – that means the lender has wired the loan amount to the escrow company. The escrow company can then pay off the seller's current mortgage, and escrow will send the signed loan documents to be recorded with the county. This all happens within the same day, and by the end of the day it should be recorded with your name as the new homeowner! At that time the transaction is considered closed!

84

Will you contact me after closing?

I do stay in touch with my clients after closing. Our relationship doesn't end there. If I think you may benefit by refinancing, I'll contact you and suggest we look at it. You'll be invited to client events, and I will be here to answer any lending/real estate questions you have, whenever you have them. My hope is that my clients had such a great experience they will refer me to others whenever they hear of someone needing mortgage help.

85

When is my first mortgage payment?

Your first mortgage payment will be due one full month after the last day of the month in which your mortgage closed. For example, if you close May15 or May 29, your first mortgage payment is due on July 1. There is usually a grace period until the fifteenth of the month. After that, you'll incur a late fee. If you are thirty days late it will show on your credit report.

86

When should I refinance my mortgage?

People refinance to lower their interest rate, remove mortgage insurance if they have enough equity, or maybe to pull some cash out to pay off debts, to remodel, or get cash for any reason. I stay in touch with my clients, letting them know when I think it's worth checking into refinancing. If it is not enough of a benefit, we will wait until the value has increased further.

87

Do you have relatives in trouble?

Financially that is! Reach out to me. Sometimes I hear from a past client whose sister is working with a lender and something just doesn't sound right. I can give my thoughts or even a second opinion if the sister is open to it. I'm here for any questions you have, whether for you or a relative or friend.

88

Who can I refer you to?

If you are in Western Washington, please don't hesitate to contact me if you need a bookkeeper, CPA, insurance agent, realtor, bakery, and on and on! I am active in my community in several networking groups as well as local chambers of commerce. If you need something, I most likely know and trust someone who can help you and provide excellent service. Let me know how I can assist!

They're Homeowners Now – What They Learned

Hear from my most recent homebuyer!

"We moved to the Seattle area two years ago, from a market where homes were less than half the cost. We struggled with sticker shock and saving money for the down payment took much longer than we anticipated. However, we kept saving what we could. We just closed on our home last week and it feels great knowing that we accomplished our goal of becoming homeowners in the Pacific Northwest!" -- *Natalie Bollinger*

90

Buying a new home after divorce.

"Buying a home after divorce is scary, but so was getting divorced. Buying my home made me feel strong and empowered as a single mom. Having a lender who is there to help when you need them.is invaluable. Have an attitude that surprises will come, and be prepared to roll with the punches. Don't let opinions of others be a deciding factor for you or try to make them happy!" --*Deann B.*

91

Refinancing helped this mom start over.

"After a rough few years I was at a very low, overwhelming point in my life. Bills hanging over my head, a large mortgage; I felt like I couldn't breathe. In came Lynn with a, "Let's give it a try" attitude. Surprisingly, my credit was good and a refinance made total sense. Sometimes we feel like we can't do it, but Lynn is there to walk you through it." --*Robin Monillas*

92

There's hope after bankruptcy and foreclosure.

"With low credit scores, a bankruptcy and foreclosure in our past, we never thought we'd be able to purchase another home to raise our two boys. We contacted Lynn and she guided us on what to do to become homeowners again. We were oblivious to all the different loans and criteria but from start to finish, we were in our new home in six months!" --*F. Potts*

93

Single moms can make it happen!

"Being a single mom of three and starting over wasn't on my agenda, but my ultimate goal was to have my own house. My mortgage lender told me 'no' for three years due to credit issues. Finally Lynn told me to go look! Purchasing MY home was the best feeling ever. It discounted all negative thoughts from myself and others. Get what's yours. Home is where the heart is!" --*Mary Thoreson*

94

Starting over making dreams come true!

"I wasn't sure where to start since my ex-husband had controlled all our finances. I felt a little embarrassed discussing my lack of freedom in basic financial decisions in my marriage. Lynn made me feel at ease, and I trusted her. I began to feel a sense of relief and excitement, thinking, "Could this really happen?". When the day finally came to sign the papers, I was elated!"—*Beth L, local business owner*

95

Personal favorite – she didn't give up!

"I was a single parent, raising two grandkids. I feared I wouldn't qualify. After almost a year to start the process, once pre-approved, I had to find something I could afford. There was disappointment, but about a year later, I found a house in a perfect neighborhood. I will never forget the overwhelming mixture of emotions I felt telling my family we owned a house-- intense joy and accomplishment." *-J. Mason*

96

Sometimes it does take a village.

I helped a widow buy a new home on her own. It was clear she was still in mourning and moving into a place of her own was very hard. Fortunately her family was looking out for her, and her daughter-in-law was a mortgage lender in another state. I talked with her and she reassured my client's family that the selected loan program was correct for her and she was in good hands.

97

The fourth time was the charm.

"My husband and I had tried to buy our first home three different times. It always fell through for one reason or another; the most recent due to the lender dropping the ball. This time, we spoke to at least four lenders before deciding that Lynn was the most supportive, helpful and communicative by far. It was a no-brainer. She made the process painless, was with us every step of the way, and closed us two weeks early!" *--Anonymous*

98

She didn't think it could happen.

"Lynn was recommended by our Realtor after our first lending attempt fell flat. Lynn was there every step of the way sharing her wealth of knowledge and helping us find the perfect loan. Lynn was organized, professional, transparent and quick to respond to all our questions. I highly recommend Lynn to everyone looking to buy a home. She's extremely genuine and personable and provided us with the best possible service." --*S. Perry*

99

It doesn't have to be stressful.

"I cannot begin to recommend Lynn enough! She was incredibly patient with us, answered every question knowledgeably, and she was so quick with getting back to us. Going through a mortgage process can be stressful, but we felt so supported by Lynn and she took that stress away. I have told all of my family and friends about Lynn and we will certainly use her in the future."
--*N. Closser*

100

A final lesson to take away

Our fears keep us from doing things we really want to do. We're afraid of reaching out for the answers we need, staying paralyzed rather than taking action. We miss out on so much by doing this! When I'm unsure I'll ask myself: What's the worst that could happen if I just give it a shot? It's almost always worth trying, don't you think? Maybe you can buy *your* own home sooner than you think!

~ Contact Lynn Reifert ~

Email:

FearFreeMortgage@gmail.com

Facebook:

Facebook.com/LynnReifert

Instagram:

TakingTheFearOutOfMortgages

LinkedIn:

Linkedin.com/in/lynnreifert/

Apply online:

LynnReifert.com

Licensed in several states

Thank you to my coaching accountability partner Leslie Madsen of Keller Williams. Thanks for your thoughts and opinions on cover photo, color, etc. I really appreciate your time, you're the best!

Jessica Butts, Debra Trappen and Debbie Page*:*

All three of you were integral in helping me recognize that I already had my 'niche' – I just needed to develop it. I'm blessed to have such talented and inspirational women to connect with and learn from – thank YOU!

Allie Lord, Laney Shorett and Jolene Messmer

All three of you helped me to get to the place I am today. Allie hired me as her assistant in 2008. I learned grace and generosity in action from her – to this day. Laney, from you I learned I didn't have to create a big presentation when meeting agents. I learned to just be myself and see if there's a connection. Because of this I can honestly say that I truly enjoy the agents I work with. Jolene, you are never too busy to give me a little rah-rah or help me see a situation from another perspective. Thank you all for being great examples of strong women loan officers and strong women in general! Love you all!

About the *Six-Word Lessons Series*

Legend has it that Ernest Hemingway was challenged to write a story using only - six words. He responded with the story, "For sale: baby shoes, never worn." The story tickles the imagination. Why were the shoes never worn? The answers are left up to the reader's imagination.

This style of writing has a number of aliases: postcard fiction, flash fiction, and micro fiction. Lonnie Pacelli was introduced to this concept in 2009 by a friend, and started thinking about how this extreme brevity could apply to today's communication culture of text messages, tweets and Facebook posts. He wrote the first book, *Six-Word Lessons for Project Managers*, then started helping other authors write and publish their own books in the series.

The books all have six-word chapters with six-word lesson titles, each followed by a one-page description. They can be written by entrepreneurs who want to promote their businesses, or anyone with a message to share.

See the entire *Six-Word Lessons Series* at **6wordlessons.com**